START-A-CRAFT

Toleware

Get started in a new craft with easy-to-follow

projects for beginners

ANN WITCHELL

APPLE

A QUINTET BOOK

Published by The Apple Press
6 Blundell Street
London N7 9BH

ISBN 1-85076-692-4

This book was designed and produced by
Quintet Publishing Limited
6 Blundell Street
London N7 9BH

Creative Director: Richard Dewing
Designer: James Lawrence
Project Editor: Coral Walker
Photographer: Paul Forrester

Typeset in Great Britain by
Central Southern Typesetters, Eastbourne
Manufactured in Singapore by Eray Scan Pte Ltd
Printed in China by Leefung-Asco Printers Ltd

DEDICATION

**In memory of Garfield, and with love and
thanks to Eric and to my teachers and
mentors Tahira Lewis, Belinda Ballantine
and Sally Richmond.**

Many thanks to Young and D for tinware,
the Decorative Arts Co Limited for tinware,
paint and art supplies.

CONTENTS

INTRODUCTION

Since its introduction in the early 18th century, painted tinware has been a popular – if not perhaps much publicized – craft. The name toleware originates from the French *la tole peinte* (painted tin) and it was the French, among other European manufacturers, who developed very sophisticated toleware or "japanning" to imitate the exquisite lacquerware being imported in the late 17th and early 18th centuries from Japan. Beautiful pieces were produced at this time, culminating in Chippendale and lace-edged trays, painted in elegant floral designs or decorated with gold leaf.

But it was the early settlers in the United States who became the first producers of household tinware. In 1740, the Patterson brothers of Berlin, Connecticut began importing sheet tin from England to make cooking utensils. This early tinware was undecorated – largely because the New England and Pennsylvanian settlers were Puritans and deeply opposed to ornamentation of any kind. It was not until the late 18th century that this US tinware was being japanned in the manner of the European ware. The early tin was elaborately decorated by skilled workmen, trained in the techniques used abroad.

These highly decorated items were bought by rich, moneyed families. Soon however, the rural tinsmiths began to produce a type of simple painted tin, intended for quick, cheap sale. Much of this 19th century ware was marketed through stores, although more of it was sold by pedlars, at first by foot and later by cart as these travelling salesmen made ever longer reaching journeys.

The country tinsmiths decorated their tin with brushstroke painting which all apprentice decorators learnt. The painted household objects were various: trays, cookie boxes, pitchers, canisters, coffee pots and trinket boxes. The American housewife was quick to seize upon these bright new items to cheer her home after years of dull tin and pewter.

Today, we can recapture the pleasure of those early artists and the housewives who bought their wares by creating colourful and personal accessories to grace our own homes.

BASIC EQUIPMENT AND MATERIALS

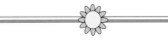

PAINTS

Water-based acrylic paints and primers have been used for all the projects contained in this book because of their ease of application, quick-drying properties, absence of toxic substances, and also because brushes and containers can easily be cleaned with mild detergent and water.

Until recently it was felt preferable to use oil-based products on tinware because of the non-absorbency of the surface and because painted surfaces on tin tend to chip more easily. However, the phasing out of oil- or solvent-based products has brought water-based versions to the fore, and advances in paint manufacturing mean that acrylic primers and paints are now available for painting toleware successfully.

PRIMERS

There are two types of primer, one for galvanized or zinc-plated tin, and one for non-ferrous metals, (brass and copper, etc). The majority of tin items fall into the galvanized category.

BASECOATS

Acrylic paints in large containers can be bought from art shops and suppliers. **Emulsion paints**, which can be used as basecoats for wooden items are not suitable for painting on to tinware. These paints adhere to surfaces by sinking into them, which they cannot do with metal.

Oil-based basecoats can be used but they must be applied on top of an oil-based primer. Brushes should be cleaned in turpentine or white spirit. However, oil-based paint and water-based paint do not sit happily together, so if you wish to paint your design in acrylics you will need to paint a coat of shellac or sanding sealer over the dry basecoat. Once this, in turn, is dry you can paint your design in acrylics.

Enamel paints can be used on metal and give a glossy, lacquer-like finish which is similar to "japanned" articles. These paints are oil-based, so once again a coat of shellac or sanding sealer will be needed to isolate the basecoat from your acrylic designs.

Finally, cellulose metal paints and **car spray paints** can be used. They are compatible with acrylics and the design can be painted directly on to these finishes.

DESIGN PAINTS

Acrylics can be purchased in tubes or jars – the latter being preferable for brushstroke work as they are more fluid. There is a huge variety of colours from which to choose or they can be mixed. They can be thinned with water to a looser consistency when needed, as in liner or script work. Brushes are washed in soapy water to clean them.

OTHER MATERIALS

RUST INHIBITOR

A proprietary "paint" that contains chemicals to seal in and prevent further rusting. It is available from hardware or DIY stores. You will need this if you are preparing old, rusty tinware.

SHELLAC, SANDING SEALER AND WHITE POLISH

These products seal and protect. They are available from specialist suppliers. They are solvent-based, quick-drying, and are compatible with both oil-based and water-based preparations. Wash brushes in methylated spirit.

METHYLATED SPIRIT

Widely available, methylated spirit has many uses. Apart from cleaning brushes, it can remove acrylic and water-based paints from surfaces – either where paint has been spilt accidentally or where the intention is to remove paint as an antiquing or distressing device.

GOLD LEAF

Gold leaf can be real gold (very expensive), or Dutch metal leaf which is more economical and has been used for the projects in this book. It is available as loose leaf or transfer leaf. The transfer leaf is the easiest to handle as it is on a backing paper. Try not to touch the metal leaf more than you need to because it can be marked very easily. Unlike real gold leaf, Dutch metal leaf will tarnish and needs to be varnished or lacquered to prevent this.

BRONZE POWDERS

Bronze powders are fine metallic powders made from copper, silver, aluminium or alloys. They too need to be protected with varnish or lacquer.

GOLD SIZE

Gold size is used in gilding to adhere the metal leaf to the surface and is available in many different drying times ranging from 30 minutes to 24 hours. 3-hour gold size has been used on the gilded projects in this book.

VARNISHES

Oil-based and water-based varnishes are available and both can be used over your projects whether the design work is in oils or acrylics. The only time you must be sure to use oil-based varnish is with crackle varnishing.

Oil-based varnishes take a long time to dry, 24 hours or longer, and can "yellow" your colours because of the linseed oil content. Water-based varnishes dry very quickly which means that you can apply several coats in a day, if you wish. As they contain no oil, they will not yellow with age.

You can also buy special **crackle-varnish** kits. These contain one oil-based varnish, which is applied first, then a water-based varnish, which is coated on top of the nearly dry oil-based varnish. The result is an aged, distressed appearance to the item being decorated.

BRUSHES AND APPLICATORS

OTHER EQUIPMENT

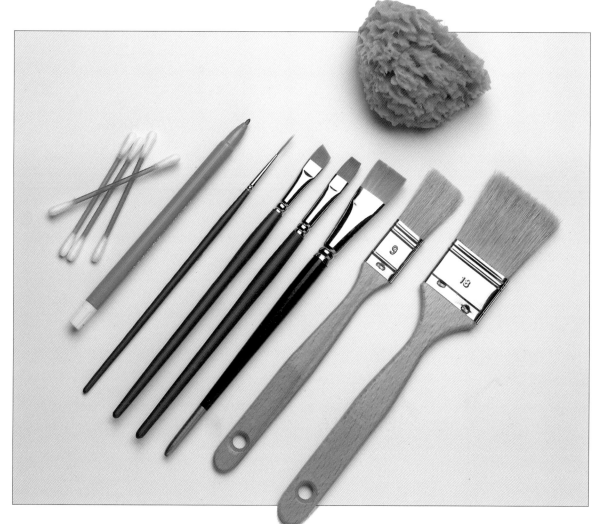

WIRE BRUSH

Useful for brushing off flaking rust on old tin items in readiness for washing and applying a rust inhibitor.

SANDPAPER

The coarser grades of sandpaper are needed to sand down enamel-painted items before priming. The finer grades of sandpaper can be used between coats of varnish.

Chalk is useful when positioning your design on larger objects.

PAPERS

Tracing paper is used for tracing designs and patterns. To transfer the designs you will need tracing-down paper. This wax-free carbon-paper comes in a variety of colours, (white, yellow, blue, black), and can be removed with an eraser. It is used in conjunction with tracing paper to transfer the design on to the item you are decorating. Trace-down should not be confused with ordinary carbon-paper. New varieties coming on to the market include papers whose traces disappear when painted over.

MASKING TAPE

Used for either holding the tracing and transfer papers when applying a design, or for isolating adjoining areas when painting, the masking tape you use needs to be "low-tack". If the adhesive on the tape is too sticky it may pull off the paint when removed.

Brushes cover a huge range in design, type and price. For decorative painting they fall into two types: base-coating or varnishing brushes and design brushes.

VARNISH BRUSHES

Varnish brushes are flat and can be bought in a variety of sizes. The 2cm (1in) and 4cm (1⅛in) sizes are most useful for small items and can be used for primers, basecoats and varnishes. Inexpensive ½cm (⅛ in) decorators' brushes are good enough for applying spirit-based products, like shellac, because the product will ruin good brushes.

DESIGN BRUSHES

Design brushes come under the heading of artists' brushes. Most of the projects in this book have been completed using "round" brushes, sizes 2 and 4. A liner or script brush is useful for fine lines or tendrils and a flat brush or angled shader can be used for heavier borders. Synthetic brushes are quite satisfactory for use with acrylics, do not be tempted to buy the expensive sable brushes.

SPONGE

A natural sponge is preferable as it will give a greater variation in pattern than a synthetic sponge. Squeeze out in water before using and never leave it soaking in harsh solvents.

STYLUS

A stylus is a multi-purpose tool. In toleware it is used when tracing designs on to objects, and it can be used for adding dots of paint to the design.

TECHNIQUES

PRIMING

The items you will find or purchase for decorating will fall into one of three categories; new tinware, old tinware or enamelled tinware, (this last type includes previously painted tinware).

The first step for any of the above will be a good wash and scrub. If the tinware is old it is probably dusty and dirty. If it is new galvanized tin it will probably have a protective oily coating which will need removing before painting. Once the item has been washed it will need drying thoroughly in case any water is in the seams. If left, this will cause rust

to break out which would eventually break through your design work. A small item could be put in the oven at a low temperature for a while. If this is not possible, stand the item in a warm place in the house for a day or two. If the item is enamelled, or has been previously painted, give it a wash to remove any dirt or grime.

Once the new metal is clean, the item will be ready for priming. If old metal, the next task is to examine the item for any rust patches or spots. If there are any, remove any loose rust by brushing with a wire brush or very coarse sandpaper. Then

treat with rust inhibitor. Once this has dried, the item will be ready for priming. If the item is enamelled or painted, give it a sand down with coarse sandpaper to form a key to which the paint can adhere.

Once the above steps have been carried out, the primer can then be applied. Check that you have the correct primer for the type of metal you are painting. Once the primer is dry, you can carry on with your base-coating. Metal often needs two basecoats; give the first coat plenty of time to dry before applying the second.

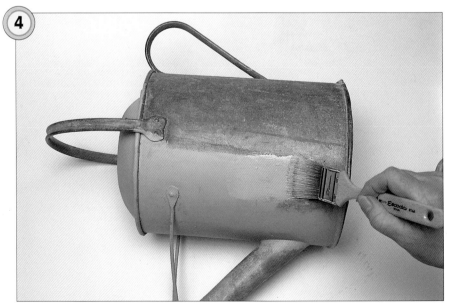

BRUSH STROKES

As mentioned in the Introduction, decorative and folk art painting are based on brushstrokes, the most common being the comma and "S" strokes. The technique for these strokes may take a little time to learn but it is well worth the time spent practising.

Comma

Using a round brush, try the comma stroke first. Hold the brush perpendicular to the paper. Gently put the whole length of the brush down on to the paper, then apply a little pressure so that the brush hairs flare out forming the rounded head of the comma. Pull the brush slowly back towards you releasing the pressure on the brush and letting the hairs return to a point. Keep pulling back towards you and lifting the brush until you come to a fine point. Stop and then lift off.

'S' stroke

The "S" stroke is like a long pulled-out letter 'S', with the beginning and end strokes heading in the same direction. Begin on the tip of the brush. Pull the brush towards you, gradually increasing pressure. Change direction, still increasing pressure, until you are halfway through the "S". Start to decrease pressure while still pulling back towards you. Change direction back to the original, and carry on lifting pressure until you are back on the tip of the brush. Stop, then lift off.

The amount of paint you need on the brush will come naturally after a while: a good rule of thumb is that the paint should reach about halfway up the hairs. Paint should be the consistency of cream, so you may need to add a little water.

The liner or script brush is used for plant tendrils and fine lines. Water the paint down to an ink-like consistency and always hold the brush in an upright position.

Stylus Dots

The stylus, or the end of the brush, can be used to put dots in the painting, (for example, flower centres). If you want the dots to be consistent, you will need to dip the stylus or brush handle in the paint each time. If you keep going with the same paint load, the dots will diminish in size.

GILDING

Some simple techniques have been used in two of the projects in this book. Full instructions have been given in each section, see pages 21 and 29.

CRACKLE GLAZE

This finish is frequently confused with crackle varnish. Crackle glaze is applied between two layers of paint. The basecoat is applied and, when dry, the crackle glaze is applied where wanted. This too is allowed to dry and then the top coat is put on. The glaze will immediately start "working" and cracking the paint. The crazing will go on for some time, so it is best to leave the item until the reaction stops, overnight is safest. With this finish, the basecoat and topcoat need to be contrasting colours in order that the coat underneath will show through when the cracking appears.

CRACKLE VARNISH

Crackle varnish works when two layers of special varnish are applied at the end of painting. Following the completion of the design work, the first oil-based coat of varnish is applied. This is left until nearly dry and then the second water-based coat is applied. This is left until dry and then heat is applied – a hairdryer works well – and the top coat of the varnish will crack. It is often difficult to see the web of cracks until the antiquing is applied, and this is done next. Mix a little Raw Umber oil paint with a drop of white spirit and, using a soft cloth, rub it all over the crackle varnish surface. Then take a piece of kitchen paper towel and wipe off the excess oil paint. The antiquing will stop in the varnish cracks and you will be able to see the crazed effect. Finish off with a coat of oil-based varnish; this coat cannot be water-based.

Always practise these effects on scrap items before applying them to your finished object.

VARNISHING

The cardinal rule of varnishing is to remember to apply the varnish sparingly. Several fine coats are better than one heavy one. It is preferable to varnish in daytime, and it should be carried out in a dry, dust-free environment. Work on a small section at a time, overlapping each section slightly. If you wish to, you can sand down after each coat of varnish with a very fine sandpaper. Always varnish your projects when completed to protect your precious work from damage and deterioration.

WATERING CAN

A second-hand discovery, a little tender loving care, and one of my favourite designs made this watering can both useful and decorative. The background foliage is simply sponged on. Don't be daunted by painting all the flowers: with a little practise, they'll flow happily from your brush.

You will need

◊ Watering can (primed and painted with dark green basecoat)
◊ Tracing paper
◊ Transfer paper
◊ Masking tape
◊ Stylus
◊ Sponge
◊ Kitchen paper towel
◊ Nos. 2 and 4 round artists' brushes
◊ No. 5/0 script artists' brush
◊ Palette or plate for paint
◊ Acrylic paints in Fawn, Antique White, Raw Umber, Hooker's Green, Ocean Green, Leaf Green and Yellow Oxide
◊ Varnish
◊ Varnish brush

1 Trace the daisy design (see page 45) on to
tracing paper and attach to the side of the watering can using masking tape. Slide transfer paper underneath the tracing paper. Trace only the dotted line on to the can.

2 Take the sponge and dampen it. To create a background of foliage for the flowers you will need to fill in the space below the traced-on dotted line with the three shades of green. First, sponge on the darkest green at the bottom of the design to a height of about 4 cm (1½ in). Blot excess paint on to kitchen paper as you work.

3 The mid-green is sponged on next and the lightest green is applied last, letting this colour run up to the dotted line. Take care not to leave a line between each colour; merge them to make the foliage look natural.

TIP
• When decorating old, secondhand tinware use a stiff wire brush to remove as much flaking metal or rust as possible. A proprietary rust inhibitor will prevent any further deterioration before painting.

4 When the paint is dry, replace the traced design, hold in place with masking tape and slide the transfer paper underneath. Now trace down the whole of the design, using the stylus, and repeat for the smaller design on the top of the can.

5 Using the Fawn paint, and a No. 4 brush, base-coat in the daisy petals.

6 Take the Raw Umber and the No. 2 brush and base-coat in the centres of the daisies.

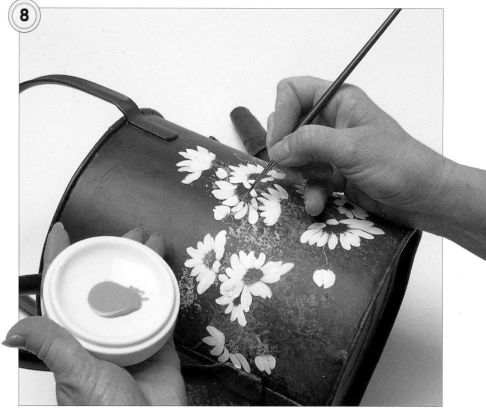

7 Now finish the daisy petals with the Antique White applied with the No. 4 brush.

8 Complete the centres of the daisies by adding highlights. Use Yellow Oxide and the No. 2 brush and pat in some colour on the part of the Raw Umber centres where the light would catch them.

9 Finish off the centres with a few random small, white dots applied with the stylus.

10 Use the very palest green to paint in the tendrils, stalks and sepals.

LANTERN

This Turkish-style lantern begged a decoration which hinted of the exotic. I felt that a midnight
blue background studded with gold and silver stars was the best way to enhance it.

You will need

◊ Lantern (primed and painted with blue
   basecoat)
◊ Sponge
◊ Kitchen paper towel
◊ Palette or plate for paint
◊ Acrylic paints in gold, silver and Yellow
   Oxide
◊ Tracing paper
◊ Transfer paper
◊ Masking tape
◊ Stylus
◊ No. 2 round artists' brush
◊ Varnish
◊ Varnish brush

TIP

• Synthetic brushes are perfectly
acceptable to use with acrylic paints
for toleware. Do not feel you must
buy expensive sable or real hair
paintbrushes.

1 Dampen the sponge and dip it into the gold
paint. Pat off any excess paint on to a piece of
paper towel and then sponge the gold on to the
lantern with light, "pouncing" movements.

2 If you are confident, you can probably paint this
simple design freehand. Alternatively, trace the
design on page 46 on to tracing paper and then,
holding the tracing in place with masking tape, slide
the transfer paper underneath. Transfer the design
on to the lantern, using the stylus.

3 With the artists' brush, paint in the silver, six-pointed stars.

4 To create a sparkling shooting star trail, use the stylus and the silver paint to
add a sweeping curve of dots for each silver star.

5 For the golden, four-pointed stars, basecoat in the shapes with the Yellow Oxide and the No. 2 brush. Leave to dry.

6 Rinse out the brush and, with the gold paint, paint over the Yellow Oxide to complete the four-pointed stars. Make sure the paint is completely dry before applying a coat of varnish.

SET OF PITCHERS

A favourite design of mine, and one which is based on an early 19th century French pattern. The design is modified for the different sizes of the pitchers and is painted over a basecoat, devised specially to create an old, aged appearance.

You will need
◊ Set of pitchers (primed, ready for basecoats)
◊ Basecoats in Deep Orange and Brown Umber
◊ Brush to apply basecoats
◊ Tracing paper
◊ Transfer paper
◊ Masking tape
◊ Stylus
◊ No. 5/0 script artists' brush
◊ Nos. 2 and 4 round artists' brushes
◊ No. 4 flat brush
◊ Palette or plate for paint
◊ Acrylic paints in Burnt Umber, Leaf Green, Antique Gold, Bonnie Blue, Persimmon, Antique White and Hooker's Green
◊ Varnish
◊ Varnish brush

TIP
• Do not skimp with preparation: apply two basecoats to the metal before decoration, allowing the first coat adequate time to dry before applying the second.

1 Before beginning the design, paint the pitchers with a Deep Orange basecoat and then apply a Brown Umber wash (50:50 paint:water) over the top. Leave to dry.

2 Trace the designs (on page 46) on to tracing paper and, selecting the appropriate design for the size of your pitcher, attach it to the side with masking tape. Slide the transfer paper underneath the tracing paper and transfer the design with the stylus.

3 Using the script brush, paint in the stalks in Burnt Umber.

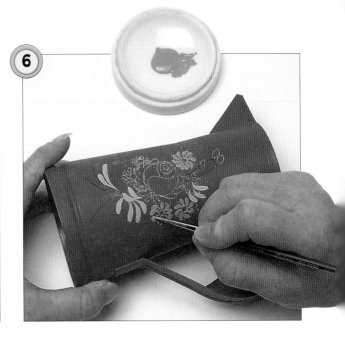

4 Thoroughly rinse the script brush, and paint in the rosebud stalks with Hooker's Green.

5 Paint in the leaves using the Leaf Green and the No. 2 brush.

6 Rinse the No. 2 brush and paint in the petals on the pinwheel daisies with Bonnie Blue.

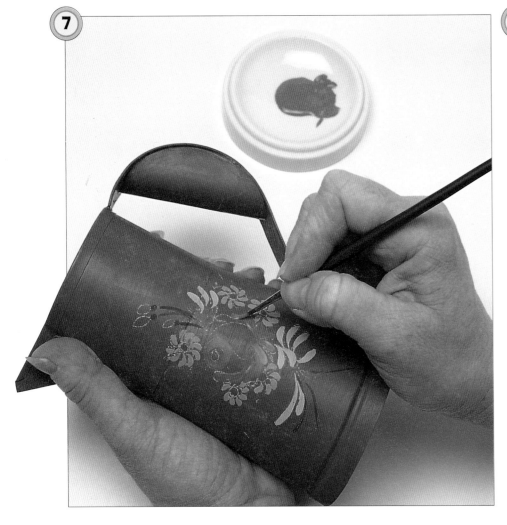

7 Using the No. 4 brush, and the Persimmon, paint in the base petals of the rose, the heart of the rose, and the rosebuds.

8 Take the Burnt Umber and apply with the No. 2 brush to paint in the centre of the rose and the centres of the pinwheel daisies.

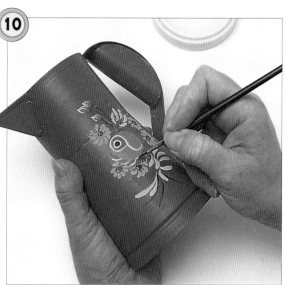

9 Put some Persimmon paint in your palette and add some white to create a paler red. Use this colour and the No. 4 brush to paint in the bowl of the rose.

10 Complete the design by adding highlights to the daisy centres, the rose and the rosebuds, using Antique White and the No. 2 brush.

11 These pitchers are offset by a burnished-style golden rim. Use the No. 4 flat brush and the Antique Gold to paint the top and bottom of the pitcher, and to rim the edges of the handle. When the paint is completely dry, apply a coat of varnish.

WATER FOUNTAIN

This novel fountain is designed for washing soiled and muddy hands in the garden or outhouse. I pictured it in an old country-style garden, so decided to give it a crackled-painted effect for an aged and well-worn look. The trailing, overgrown ivy complements the garden theme.

You will need

◊ Water fountain (primed and painted with pink basecoat)
◊ Chalk
◊ Crackle glaze
◊ Brush to apply glaze
◊ Contrasting topcoat – we have used cream
◊ Brush for applying the topcoat
◊ Tracing paper
◊ Transfer paper
◊ Stylus
◊ No. 5/0 script artists' brush
◊ Nos. 2 and 4 artists' brushes
◊ Palette or plate for paint
◊ Acrylic paints in Hooker's Green, Ocean Green, Salem Green, Leaf Green, Antique White, Fawn and Raw Umber
◊ Varnish
◊ Varnish brush

1 Choose the areas where you want the paint to crackle and outline them with chalk. Apply crackle-glaze to these areas. Leave to dry.

2 Apply the top, contrasting, coat of cream-coloured paint to the whole fountain. When going over the crackle-glazed areas, paint lightly and use only one or two strokes. If overworked, the crackle-glaze will not craze correctly.

TIP
• Some of the solvents recommended for cleaning brushes used for oil-based paints or varnishes are expensive. It would be more economical to use a cheap brush and discard after use.

3 Leave the container to dry, preferably overnight. The crackle glaze will start to work immediately, cracking the paint, and you will find this will continue for some time.

4 Trace the trailing ivy design (see page 47) on to the tracing paper. Attach these to the container with masking tape and, sliding the transfer paper under the tracing paper, transfer the designs with the stylus. At this point, transfer only the outline of the leaves and not the veins.

5 Using the No. 4 brush, paint in the leaves using the Hooker's Green for the leaves marked A on the design; Ocean Green for the leaves marked B, Salem Green for the leaves marked C and Leaf Green for the underleaf areas marked D. Leave to dry.

6 Replace the traced designs, attach with masking tape and slide the transfer paper under the tracing paper. Transfer the veins on to the leaves. Using the script brush, paint in the veins using Leaf Green.

7 To complete the design, paint the roots in Raw Umber, and the tendrils in Hooker's Green, once again using the script brush. When dry, apply a coat of varnish.

GILDED TRAY

This project gives you the opportunity to try your hand at using gold leaf. The combination of black and gold provides such a rich and opulent finish. Here, I have used a Russian technique with an early American pattern.

You will need
◊ Tray (primed and painted black)
◊ Transfer Dutch metal leaf
◊ Gold size
◊ Brush to apply size
◊ Cotton
◊ Shellac or sanding sealer
◊ Brush to apply shellac
◊ Tracing paper
◊ Transfer paper
◊ Stylus
◊ Masking tape
◊ Nos. 2 and 4 round artists' brushes
◊ No. 5/0 script artists' brush
◊ Palette or plate for paint
◊ Acrylic paints in Black, Turquoise and Yellow Oxide
◊ White polish
◊ Brush to apply polish
◊ Soft cloth

1 Apply a coat of gold size to the centre of the tray where the gold leaf is to be laid. Follow the picture here as a guide.

2 Test for tack with your knuckle; it should have the same stickiness as adhesive tape.

TIP

• Unlike real gold leaf, Dutch metal leaf is less expensive, but it will tarnish and a coat of shellac will be required to prevent this.

3 Take a sheet of transfer Dutch metal leaf and, holding it by the backing paper, lay it carefully on to the tray.

4 Before removing the backing paper, rub your fingers over the metal leaf to make sure it is stuck down and that there are no bubbles. Then remove the backing paper. When applying the next piece, overlap the first piece by about ½ cm (¼ in).

5 Repeat steps 1 and 2 when going round the edges of the tray, but cut the metal leaf into small strips, overlapping the pieces as you apply them. Leave overnight.

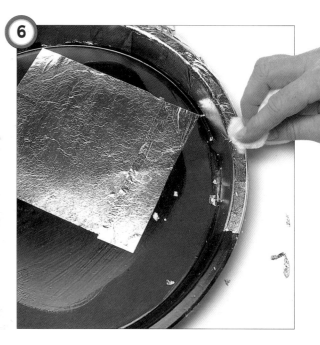

6 Next day, take a piece of cotton and gently rub over the tray, removing any loose leaf. Paint with a coat of shellac or sanding sealer.

7 Trace the design on page 48 on to tracing paper and attach to the tray with masking tape. Slide the transfer paper underneath and trace down the design with the stylus.

8 Paint in the background of the design with black paint using the No. 4 brush.

9 Paint in any fine lines with the script brush.

10 Using the No. 2 brush, paint in the detail on the large flowers. Now take the Script brush and paint the tendrils in Turquoise. Use the Turquoise also to edge the lower leaves on the border of the tray.

11 Using the No. 2 brush, finish with a little Yellow Oxide to the edges of the buds. Give the tray an application of white polish and buff with a soft cloth.

NAPKIN HOLDER

This deep blue napkin holder has been picked out with a pretty white lacy design – the perfect complement to a table laid with fine linen or damask. The technique of painting lace, perfected by the Australian decorative artists, is one of my favourite creative ideas.

You will need
◊ Napkin holder (primed and painted in dark blue basecoat)
◊ Tracing paper
◊ Transfer paper
◊ Stylus
◊ Masking tape
◊ Palette or plate for paint
◊ No. 2 round artists' brush
◊ Acrylic paint in Antique White
◊ Varnish
◊ Varnish brush

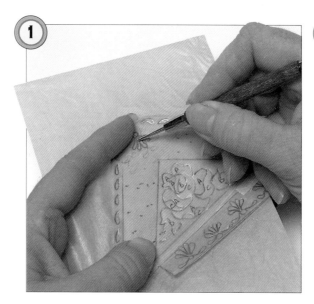

1 Trace the lacy design on page 48 on to a piece of tracing paper. Transfer on to the napkin holder with the transfer paper.

2 Mix the Antique White with some water to give a thin wash. Apply this to the front of the holder.

TIP

• Do not overload the brush with paint. A good rule of thumb is that the paint should reach halfway up the hairs.

3 With the No. 2 brush and the Antique White, apply another wash over the rose and the areas marked B.

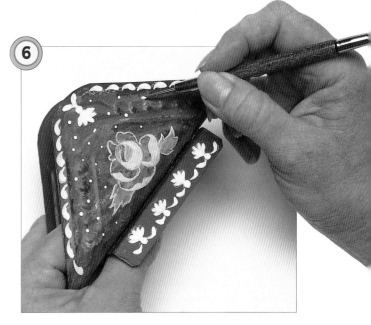

4 Paint in a final wash over the parts marked C. Leave to dry.

5 Discard the wash and return to using the Antique White paint undiluted. Paint in the commas around the edge with a No. 2 brush. This creates a lacy trim to the napkin holder.

6 Finally, randomly drop in some dots of white with the stylus. This completes the lacy impression of the design. When the piece is completely dry, coat it with varnish.

TIN TRUNK

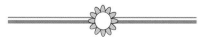

Antiqued with crackle varnish, this quaint little storage trunk has been decorated with a Swedish-inspired cream and blue design. The colours work so well because the various shades of blue harmonize beautifully together.

You will need
◊ Trunk (primed)
◊ Basecoats in cream and blue
◊ Brush to apply basecoats
◊ Old toothbrush
◊ Paper towel
◊ Tracing paper
◊ Transfer paper
◊ Masking tape
◊ Stylus
◊ No. 5/0 script artists' brush
◊ No. 4 round artists' brush
◊ Palette or plate for paint
◊ Acrylic paints in Adriatic Blue, Bonnie Blue, Blue Wisp and Cape Cod Blue
◊ Two-part crackle varnish
◊ Brushes to apply crackle varnish
◊ Tube of raw umber oil paint
◊ White spirits
◊ Soft cloth
◊ Oil-based varnish
◊ Varnish brush

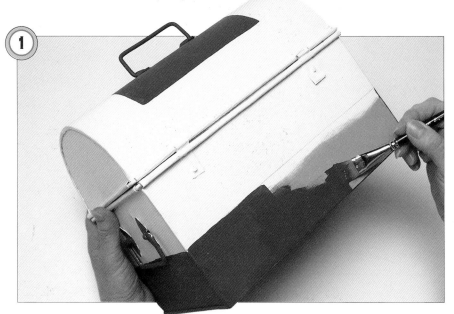

1 Measure about halfway up the sides of the trunk and mark with chalk or pencil. Paint in contrasting colours, as shown here.

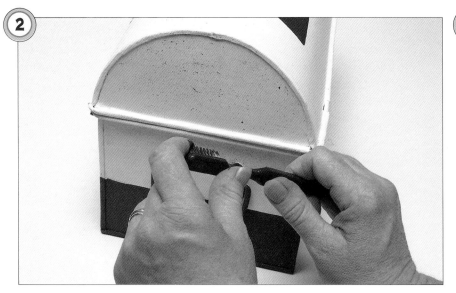

2 Using the darker colour and an old toothbrush, spatter the top, lighter half of the trunk. Spatter by dipping the toothbrush in some watered-down paint, dabbing off the excess on some paper towel and then running your finger along the brush. Practise before using on the piece you are painting.

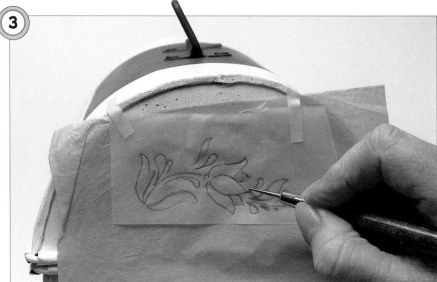

3 Trace off the design shown on page 46 on to tracing paper and attach it to the trunk. Slide the transfer paper underneath and transfer the design on to the front and sides.

4 Paint in the smallest leaves and the stalks in Adriatic Blue, using the No. 4 brush for the leaves and the script brush for the stalks.

5 Paint in the larger leaves in Bonnie Blue.

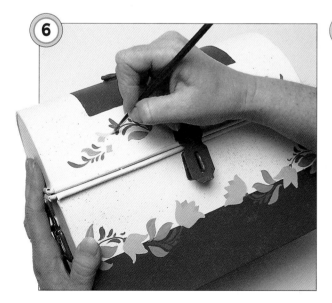

6 Paint the tulips with Blue Wisp.

7 Paint the commas on to the tulips using Cape Cod Blue.

8 Paint the trunk with the first coat of the crackle varnish and leave until the varnish is nearly dry.

9 Test to see if the varnish is ready for the second coat to go on: press it lightly with your fingers. It should feel almost dry but with a slight stickiness. Apply the second coat and allow to dry, preferably overnight. Apply heat with a hairdryer; a web of cracks will appear but will be difficult to see until the Raw Umber is applied.

10 Mix some Raw Umber oil paint with a drop of white spirits and rub on to the trunk. Take a piece of paper towel and rub off the excess. Varnish with oil-based varnish.

TIP

• If the crackle varnish does not turn out as you hoped, remove the top, water-based coat by washing it off. You can then start again with the first coat of varnish without damaging the underlying painting.

BOX OF FRUITS

A simple technique which makes use of bronze powders. The wonderful lustre of these metallic powders lifts any design from the ordinary to the special. I have based the motif on an early New England pattern.

You will need

◊ Round tin (primed and then painted in black paint)
◊ Tracing paper
◊ Transfer paper
◊ Masking tape
◊ Stylus
◊ Gold size
◊ Small, old brush to apply the size
◊ White spirits
◊ Bronze powders in gold, bronze and antique bronze
◊ No. 4 round and No. 4 flat artists' brushes
◊ Any large, soft brush
◊ Cotton
◊ Palette or plate for paint
◊ Acrylic paints in Salem Green, English Yew Green, Adobe Red, Straw, Leaf Green, Plum and Antique Rose
◊ Varnish
◊ Varnish brush

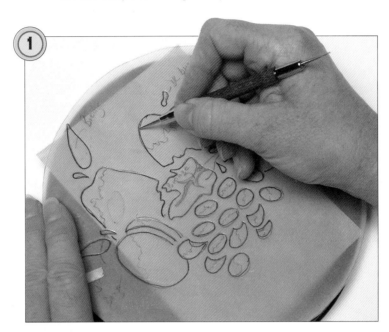

1 Trace the fruit on page 48 on to tracing paper and attach this to the side and lid of the tin with masking tape. Slide transfer paper underneath and transfer the design on to the tin using the stylus.

2 Paint the gold size sparingly into the smaller areas of the fruit marked off by the dotted lines. Leave for 5 minutes to "set". While you are waiting, clean the brush in white spirits.

3 Take the large, soft brush and dust bronze powder across the sized areas of the cherries on the side of the tin. Leave for about an hour and then dampen some cotton and wipe off the excess powder.

4 Now turn to the lid. Apply size as in Step 2. Using the large, soft brush, dust the antique bronze powder on the leaves and stalks. Do the same with the gold powder on the fruit. Leave for an hour and then dampen some cotton and wipe off the excess powder.

5 Using the No. 4 round brush, paint in the first washes of colour (50 per cent water, 50 per cent paint) on the fruit; pat the colour in roughly to make a textured finish. When dry, give a second coat, in the same way as you did the first.

6 Paint in the leaves and stalks on the border in normal, undiluted colours using Salem Green, English Yew Green and Leaf Green.

7 Take the No. 4 flat brush and paint a border around the lid with the Adobe Red. Varnish the tin when it is completely dry.

UMBRELLA STAND

A florist's vase gave me the idea for an umbrella stand. An immensely practical yet decorative item for any lobby area. The decorative bands are adapted from a design used on an antique New England tray.

You will need

◊ Container (primed and painted with khaki green basecoat)
◊ Tracing paper
◊ Transfer paper
◊ Masking tape
◊ Stylus
◊ Chalk and ruler
◊ Nos. 2 and 4 round artists' brushes
◊ No. 5/0 script artists' brush
◊ Palette or plate for paint
◊ Acrylic paints in Adobe Red, Straw, Leaf Green, Salem Green, Cayenne, Putty, Burnt Umber and Antique Gold
◊ Varnish
◊ Varnish brush

1 To position the band and keep it level, first measure with a ruler along the container to the required place and chalk in a line.

2 Trace the design (see page 46) on to tracing paper and then attach it to the container with masking tape, using the chalk line as your guide. Slide the transfer paper under the tracing paper and transfer the design with the stylus. At this point do not trace the details on the leaves or roses.

3 Using the No. 4 brush and the Putty acrylic, paint in the beige-colour commas.

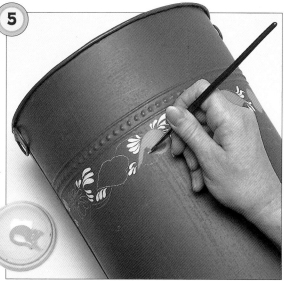

4 Now take the script brush and the Cayenne paint to describe the border lines.

5 Paint in the leaves, using Leaf Green and a No. 4 brush.

6 Thoroughly rinse the No. 4 brush and, using the Adobe Red, paint in the daisies.

7 Complete the daisies by patting in the centres using the No. 2 brush and the Antique Gold.

8 The old yellow roses are base-coated in the Straw paint. Use a No. 4 brush.

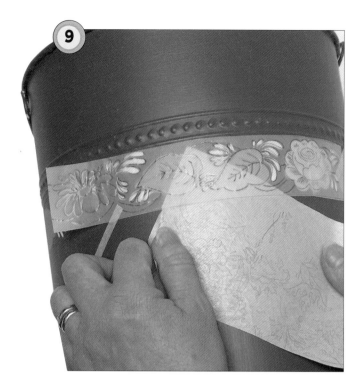

9 Take your traced design once more and reposition it over the painted areas. Slide the transfer paper underneath the design and transfer the details on to the leaves and the roses.

10 Finally, using the script brush, paint in the veins on the leaves with Salem Green and the details on the rose using Burnt Umber. When the container is completely dry, apply at least one coat of varnish.

LADLE

A nest of bluebirds in the bowl of the ladle, together with more birds and hearts decorating the handle, make this a simple but effective design for beginners to tackle. Finish the ladle with a flourish of colourful ribbons and hang it in the kitchen or family dining area.

You will need

◊ Ladle (primed and painted with cream-
   colored basecoat)
◊ Tracing paper
◊ Transfer paper
◊ Masking tape
◊ Stylus
◊ Nos. 2 and 4 round artists' brushes
◊ Palette or plate for paint
◊ Acrylic paints in Antique White, Cerulean
   Blue, Bold Red, Yellow Oxide and Black
◊ Varnish
◊ Varnish brush

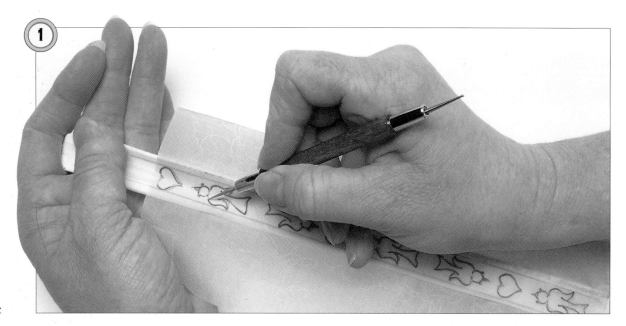

1 Transfer the three parts of the design (see page 48) on to tracing paper. Place the first part of the tracing on to the handle of the ladle using masking tape to hold it in position. Insert the transfer paper under the tracing paper and, using the stylus, copy the design on to the handle.

TIP

• Some skill is required with the paintbrush. Practise the brush strokes on a scrap of paper before you begin.

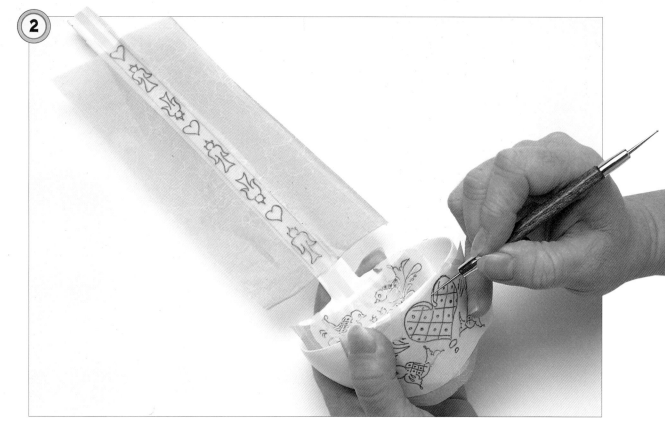

2 Transfer the other two parts of the design to the inside and outside of the bowl of the ladle, again using masking tape to hold the tracing in place and carefully sliding the transfer paper underneath the tracing paper.

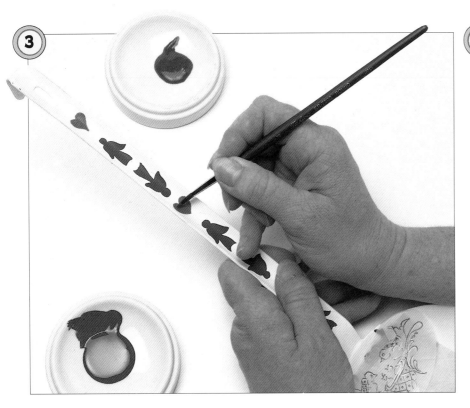

3 Work on the handle using a No. 4 brush, and paint in the bluebirds in Cerulean Blue and the little hearts in Bold Red.

4 On the bowl, paint in the bluebirds in Cerulean Blue and the heart, nest and leaves in Bold Red.

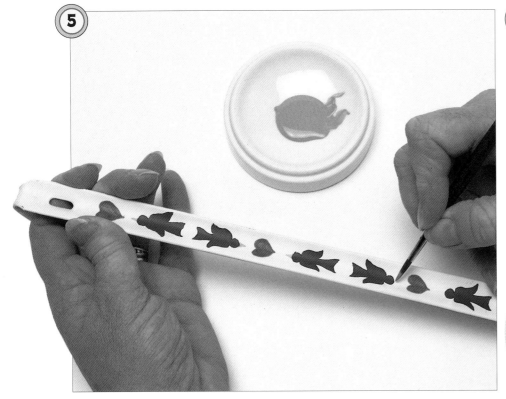

5 Acrylic paints dry very quickly, so you can now paint in the beaks of the bluebirds on both the handle and the bowl using a No. 2 brush and Yellow Oxide.

6 Mix a little Antique White with Cerulean Blue to make a pale blue and, using the No. 2 brush, paint in the lines on the wings of the bluebirds on the inside and the outside of the bowl.

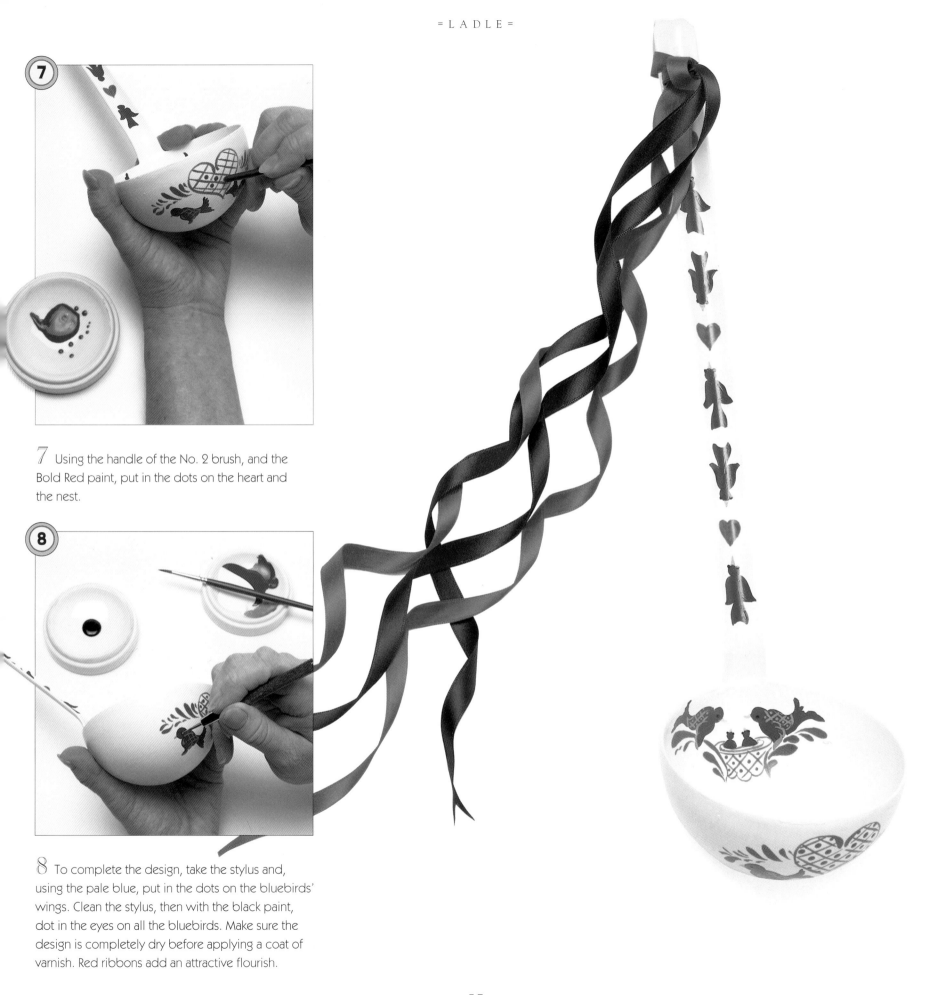

7 Using the handle of the No. 2 brush, and the Bold Red paint, put in the dots on the heart and the nest.

8 To complete the design, take the stylus and, using the pale blue, put in the dots on the bluebirds' wings. Clean the stylus, then with the black paint, dot in the eyes on all the bluebirds. Make sure the design is completely dry before applying a coat of varnish. Red ribbons add an attractive flourish.

FLAT IRON

Rescued from an old junk shop, this rusting flat iron was washed and scrubbed with a wire brush before being painted with rust inhibitor and then primed. The design is based on old-English, traditional barge painting, a naive style of strong brush strokes that can look most effective.

You will need

◊ Flat iron (primed and painted with black basecoat)
◊ Tracing paper
◊ Transfer paper
◊ Masking tape
◊ Stylus
◊ Nos. 2 and 4 round artists' brushes
◊ No. 6 flat artists' brush
◊ Palette or plate for paint
◊ Acrylic paints in Bright Green, Holly Green, Bright Red, Crimson, Antique White and Butter Yellow
◊ Varnish
◊ Varnish brush

1 Using Holly Green and the flat brush, paint the handle as indicated. Paint a green band on the base of the iron with the same brush.

2 Trace the three parts of the design for the handle, base and foot of the iron (see page 48) on to tracing paper. Using masking tape to hold the design in place, slide the transfer paper underneath the tracing paper. Trace the design on to the foot of the iron but do not trace any dotted lines at this stage.

3 Trace the leaves and daisies on to the handle and the scalloped border on to the base using the same method as described in step 2.

4 Turn the iron on its end and basecoat the roses using Crimson and a No. 4 brush. Leave to dry.

5 Replace the tracing and transfer papers to the foot of the iron and trace in the dotted lines on to the roses.

6 Using Bright Red and a No. 4 brush, paint in the rose petals with comma strokes. This will form the petals of the flower.

7 Paint the lower scalloped border on the base of the iron in Bright Red and, using the stylus, finish with an edging of white dots.

8 Work on the handle and foot of the iron, painting in green leaves with a No. 4 brush and Bright Green. Use a No. 2 brush, Antique White, and the comma stroke to paint in the daisies. Leave to dry.

9 For the decorative detail, take the Butter Yellow and apply with a No. 4 brush to add the comma strokes. Then use the No. 2 brush and the same yellow to put in the stamens on the roses. Use the stylus to add the centres of the daisies to the handle and the foot. Varnish when completely dry.

KITCHEN TIDY

This wall vase has been transformed into a handy kitchen tidy. To give it a settled-in homely look, I have antiqued it using a rubbing-down technique. This removes one layer of paint to reveal another beneath. The pattern is taken from a late 17th century biscuit box.

You will need
◊ Container (primed and then painted with contrasting basecoats)
◊ Methylated spirit
◊ Paper towel
◊ Tracing paper
◊ Transfer paper
◊ Masking tape
◊ Stylus
◊ Nos. 2 and 4 round artists' brush
◊ No. 5/0 script artists' brush
◊ Palette or plate for paint
◊ Acrylic paints in Blue Wisp, Sandstone, Adriatic Blue, Yellow Oxide, Pigskin, Blue Haze, Butter Yellow, Burnt Umber and Brown Velvet
◊ Varnish
◊ Varnish brush

1 Make a piece of paper towel into a ball and dip it into some methylated spirit. Then rub the container, using a circular motion, in the areas which you wish to look "faded". The longer you rub, the more paint will come off, exposing the contrasting paint underneath.

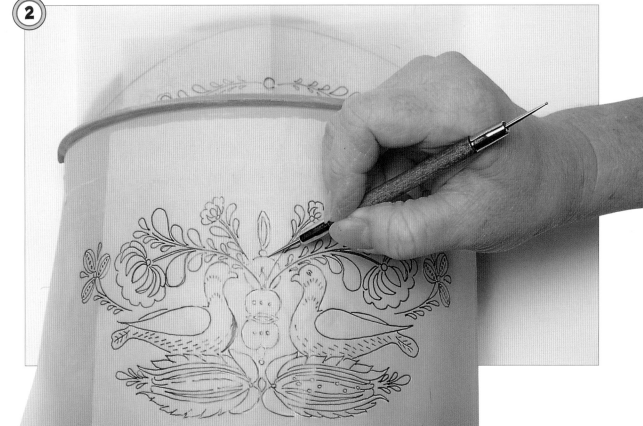

2 With the tracing paper, trace off the designs on page 45 and attach to the container with masking tape. Slide the transfer paper underneath and trace down the design with the stylus. Do not trace down the markings on the birds at this point.

3 Paint in the stalks and central design with Brown Velvet, using the script brush.

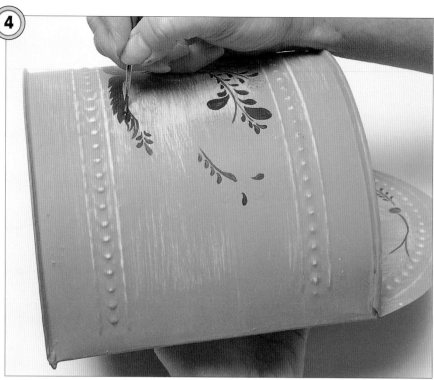

4 Use the No. 4 brush and the Burnt Umber and paint in the leaves.

5 Paint in the birds and the flowers on the back of the container. Use the No. 4 brush and Adriatic Blue and Blue Wisp.

6 Next, paint in the flowers at the edge of the design, with a No. 2 brush using Butter Yellow and Yellow Oxide.

KITCHEN TIDY

This wall vase has been transformed into a handy kitchen tidy. To give it a settled-in homely look, I have antiqued it using a rubbing-down technique. This removes one layer of paint to reveal another beneath. The pattern is taken from a late 17th century biscuit box.

You will need

◊ Container (primed and then painted with contrasting basecoats)
◊ Methylated spirit
◊ Paper towel
◊ Tracing paper
◊ Transfer paper
◊ Masking tape
◊ Stylus
◊ Nos. 2 and 4 round artists' brush
◊ No. 5/0 script artists' brush
◊ Palette or plate for paint
◊ Acrylic paints in Blue Wisp, Sandstone, Adriatic Blue, Yellow Oxide, Pigskin, Blue Haze, Butter Yellow, Burnt Umber and Brown Velvet
◊ Varnish
◊ Varnish brush

1 Make a piece of paper towel into a ball and dip it into some methylated spirit. Then rub the container, using a circular motion, in the areas which you wish to look "faded". The longer you rub, the more paint will come off, exposing the contrasting paint underneath.

2 With the tracing paper, trace off the designs on page 45 and attach to the container with masking tape. Slide the transfer paper underneath and trace down the design with the stylus. Do not trace down the markings on the birds at this point.

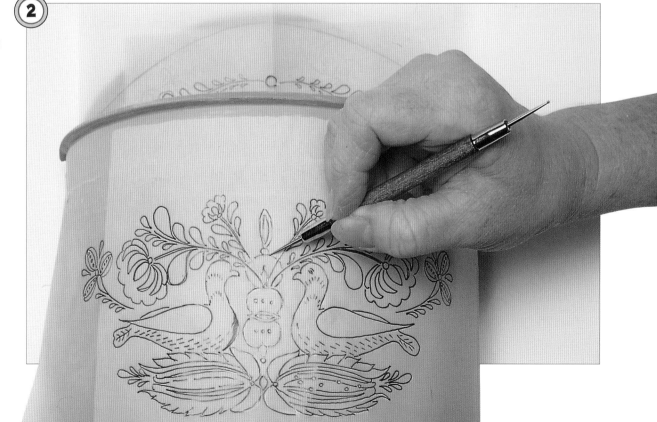

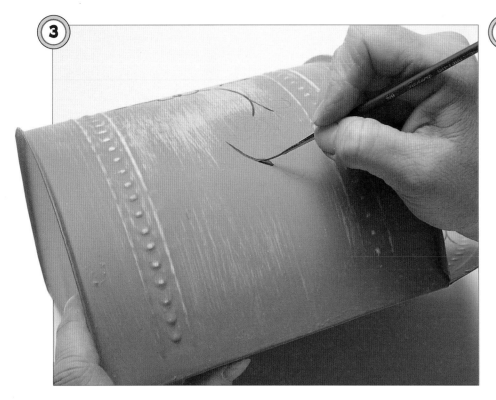

3 Paint in the stalks and central design with Brown Velvet, using the script brush.

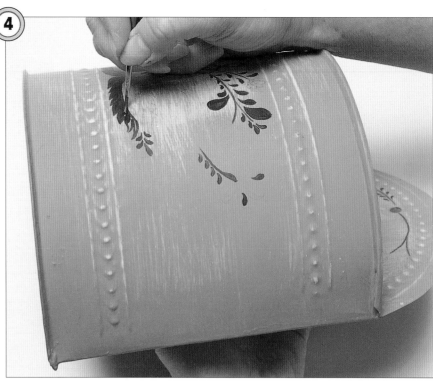

4 Use the No. 4 brush and the Burnt Umber and paint in the leaves.

5 Paint in the birds and the flowers on the back of the container. Use the No. 4 brush and Adriatic Blue and Blue Wisp.

6 Next, paint in the flowers at the edge of the design, with a No. 2 brush using Butter Yellow and Yellow Oxide.

7 Using Sandstone, paint in the larger flowers.

8 Using the No. 2 brush, paint in the sepals of the larger flowers using Pigskin.

9 Use the Blue Haze and script brush and paint in the details on the birds. Also use the Blue Haze to dab in some dots on the flowers on the back of the container. Use the stylus for this.

10 Rinse off the stylus and apply the Yellow Oxide to add some dots on the lower leaves. Varnish when completely dry.

TEMPLATES

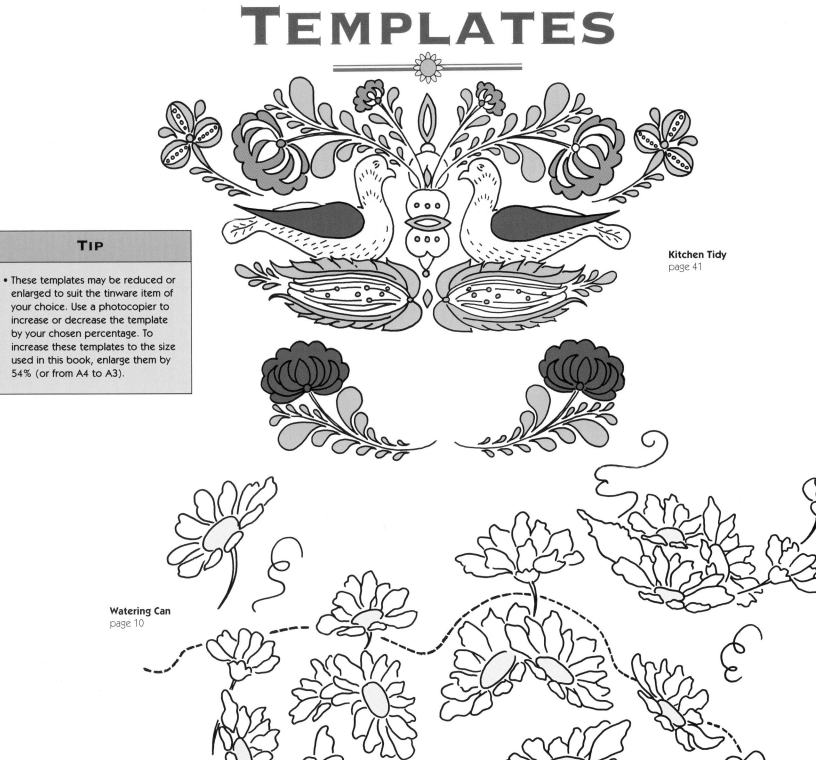

Kitchen Tidy
page 41

Watering Can
page 10

TIP

• These templates may be reduced or enlarged to suit the tinware item of your choice. Use a photocopier to increase or decrease the template by your chosen percentage. To increase these templates to the size used in this book, enlarge them by 54% (or from A4 to A3).

Umbrella Stand
page 32

Tin Trunk
page 26

Lantern
page 13

Set of Pitchers
page 15

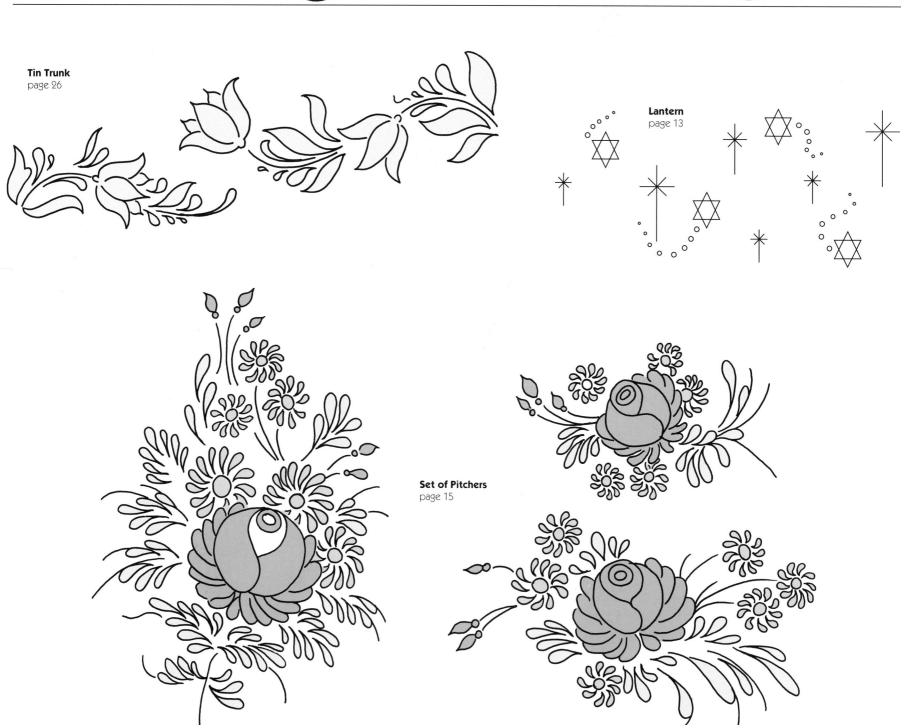

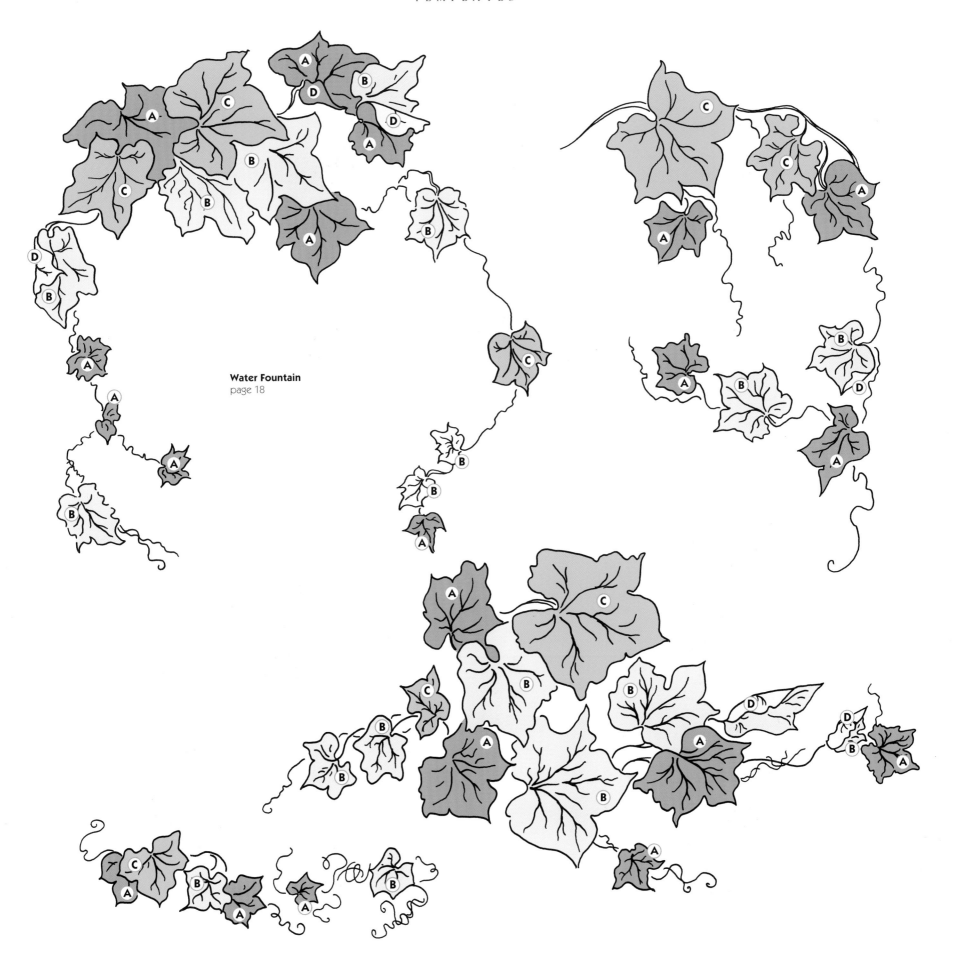

Water Fountain
page 18

Gilded Tray
page 21

Ladle
page 35

Box of Fruit
page 29

Flat Iron
page 38

Napkin Holder
page 24